Onward!
Through The Fog!

Six Dialogues Following The
Example Of Christ Through Lent

E. Morris-Pierce

Includes Worship Services
and A Tenebrae Chancel Drama

CSS Publishing Company, Inc., Lima, Ohio

ONWARD! THROUGH THE FOG!

Reprinted in 2001

Scripture quotations are from the New Revised Standard Version of the Bible, copyright 1989 by the Division of Christian Education of the National Council of the Churches of Christ in the USA. Used by permission.

Library of Congress Cataloging-in-Publication Data

Morris-Pierce, Elizabeth, 1934-
    Onward! Through the fog! : six dialogues following the example of Christ through Lent / Elizabeth Morris-Pierce
        p.   cm.
    "Includes worship services and a tenebrae chancel drama."
    ISBN 0-7880-1310-6 (pbk.)
    1. Lent. 2. Lenten sermons. 3. Drama in public worship. 4.   Worship programs. 5. Sermons, American. 6. Christian drama, American.   I. Title.
BV85.M637   1999
264—dc21   98-44906
                                                                                       CIP

ISBN 0-7880-1310-6

In dedication to pastors everywhere who creatively try to tell the "Old, Old Story" in new and different ways as they face the never-ending procession of worship services.

Table Of Contents

ASH WEDNESDAY

Ash Wednesday Worship Service

A service of meditation
and spiritual searching

Enter into the quietness of this place of worship to contemplate the Lenten journey. Allow this journey to become an opportunity for further spiritual growth. As you quietly meditate, immerse yourself in the presence of God until God's Spirit completely envelopes you and transports you far beyond normal cares and concerns. Relax and enjoy the ecstasy of your union with your God.

The Order of Worship

THE PERIOD OF QUIET MEDITATION

THE OPENING PRAYER *(in unison)*
Holy God, giver of life, what is my life apart from you? When I try to do things on my own, I discover how frail and incapable I am. And at this moment I discover how finite I am, for the first Lenten Journey ended in the death of my Savior. In remembrance of His shameful death, I acknowledge my own mortality. Forgive the sins which keep me from everlasting fellowship with you, and bring me at last to your dwelling through the mercy of Jesus, the Christ, in whose name I pray:
THE LORD'S PRAYER

THE OPENING HYMN
  "Close To Thee"

THE SCRIPTURE READINGS
  Matthew 6:1-6, 16-21
  2 Corinthians 5:20b—6:10

THE ASH WEDNESDAY MEDITATION
  "Onward! Through The Fog!"

8

THE IMPOSITION OF THE ASHES

The Invitation   Pastor

Your presence at this Ash Wednesday service gives testimony of your desire to walk with our Lord on a Lenten Journey. As we consider the example of our Lord we become aware that the Lenten Journey leads from mortality to immortality, from baser self to victory over sin.

Because of his disobedience, God told man: "I formed you from the dust of the earth, and to dust you shall return."

I invite you to receive these ashes as an acknowledgement of your mortality, and as a sincere demonstration of your desire to go forward with Christ Jesus. In these moments of silent meditation, offer your mortality to your Redeemer.

Moments of Silent Meditation

Consecration of the Ashes   Unison

Holy and Merciful God, we acknowledge you as our Creator. We live in the shadow of our mortality because of sin, but we long for immortality. Consecrate these ashes as a symbol of our origin, and consecrate your humble servants bowed before you in penitence, that by the Grace of our Lord Jesus, we may walk in newness of life. Amen.

The Hymn and Imposition of Ashes
"Have Thine Own Way, Lord"

THE SACRAMENT OF HOLY COMMUNION

The Invitation   Pastor

Jesus, our Lord, invites us to commemorate the forgiveness of sin which he won for us by his death on the cross. If you would share in this holy commemoration, bow before God and pray for his pardon.

The Prayer for Pardon   Unison

Redeeming Lord, we have acknowledged you are the source of life. We also admit you are the source of forgiveness. Pardon your penitent people who humbly bow before you. Increase our faith and instill a desire for inward purity that we may forever live with our Lord Jesus Christ. Amen.

The Prayer of Thanksgiving

L: By the grace of the Living Lord, I declare that he has forgiven you. Therefore, join in the prayer of thanksgiving.

P: **Thank you, Lord, for your forgiveness and for accepting us without condemnation. We can never thank you enough for your great mercy. Grant that we may someday be worthy to honor you with all the angels of heaven. To you be all honor and glory, now and forever. Amen.**

The Blessing of the Bread and the Cup   Pastor

Receive our prayers of gratitude, Holy Lord, and grant that we may become Christ's bread and cup to a world in need. Bless these sacred symbols of your love and forgiveness. In this sacred hour we receive the blessed bread and cup as a token of our acceptance of your sacrifice and forgiveness, and thus we honor you and your Son, our Lord. Amen.

The Sharing of the Bread and the Cup

THE HYMN OF CONSECRATION
"Lord, I Want To Be A Christian In My Heart"

THE UNISON BENEDICTION

Eternal God, we go forth from this spiritual haven with renewed resolve to serve you. Lead us onward through the weeks ahead that we may grow into your likeness and follow the example of our blessed Lord Jesus. Amen.

Ash Wednesday Meditation

ONWARD! THROUGH THE FOG!

Note: This meditation is designed to be used as a preface for the Lenten Dialogue Series: "Onward! Through The Fog!"

Introduction

Have you ever wondered how the birds find their way on their migratory flights? There are no road signs up there, and they do not read road maps; yet they reach their intended destination.

As good as the birds are in finding their way, did you know that they can become confused in a dense fog? It is not unknown for a whole formation of geese to lose their bearing in the fog and plunge headlong into tall office buildings, falling to their death on the city streets below. The birds followed their leader who had become hopelessly confused by the fog.

Most drivers have known the experience of driving at night through dense fog. If not frightening, it is at least an eerie experience. No matter how familiar you may be with each curve of the road, you become confused in the fog and discover that the curve which you thought you had reached is still several miles ahead.

If you stop, there is the worry that another driver may not see you and ram into your vehicle, and so you push ONWARD! THROUGH THE FOG!

Life is sometimes foggy

A popular item in souvenir shops and gift stores is a little plaque with those words: "ONWARD! THROUGH THE FOG!"

Unfortunately, some people live in a fog all the time and they never reach their spiritual destination. We know that we should follow Christ and his example, but it is not always an easy thing to do, for too many experiences fog up the way.

If you have been to live stage shows you have probably seen fogging devices in action. The floor is covered with fog to create the illusion that Huck Finn is steering his raft along an imaginary

11

river. In *The Phantom*, the rolling fog created an illusion of a deep abyss.

At the Tabuci Show in Branson, Misssouri, fogging devices are used in a different manner. Far above the heads of the audience, make-believe clouds roll from the fogging machine to serve as a backdrop for the laser lights as they create the effect of a huge United States flag waving above the audience. The ceiling cannot be seen, only the illusion which is created by the fog and the lights.

It's all right for a theater to create fog and distract our attention and cover up the obvious. In real life, however, there are all kinds of fog with which we must deal.

Moving on through the fog

Sometimes the fog is found in our churches, created by religious leaders who are bound up in commandments. They present so many "thou shalt not's" that they fog the path of "thou shalt." Some Christians are so busy watching what they musn't do that they lose sight of what Christ would have them do.

There is also the fog of sin, of lust, and of distractions. Wise Christians should be able to recognize the fog and push onward through it as they follow their true leader.

There is also that sneaky, insidious fog that deliberately conceals that which is above. Christian servanthood becomes concealed by the desire for recognition. Humility is fogged over and the Christian becomes dazzled by the bright lights bouncing from the clouds of honor and reward.

Spiritual rebirth must be followed by the onward and upward climb, or the believer is left to flounder in the fog of misconception. Unless Christianity changes a person, unless one becomes pure of thought and is motivated by love to serve and give, that one will become lost in the fog.

Both Jesus Christ and Saint Paul were speaking of going on to perfection in the scripture readings. There will always be something to fog our way, but we are to continue onward and upward, following Christ, our leader.

While geese may follow their leader blindly through the fog, even to their peril, we have a leader who will not lead us astray.

We can move onward through the fog with full assurance that he knows the way. Following Christ through the fog is far better than following a pair of taillights of a preceding car. We don't know where that car is going, but we DO know that in Christ we have assurance of our ultimate goal. After Lent there is the Resurrection!

This Lenten season you are invited to follow the Exemplar Christ and experience help in such areas as temptation, faith and obedience, love, meekness and strength, power and deed, and humility. Each week we will explore one of these areas.

As we prepare to follow the example of Christ through our Lenten journey, let us now bow in humility and receive the reminders of our own fraility.

Note: here may follow "The Imposition of the Ashes."

FIRST SUNDAY IN LENT

First Sunday In Lent Worship Helps
(color: Purple)

SCRIPTURES

Old Testament	Genesis 2:15-17; 3:1-7
New Testament	Romans 5:12-19
Gospel	Matthew 4:1-11
Psalter	Psalm 32

SUGGESTED HYMNS
"Grace Greater Than Our Sin" (Johnston/Towner)
"He Touched Me" (Gaither)
"It Is Well With My Soul" (Spafford/Bliss)
"O Jesus, I Have Promised" (Bode/Mann)
"Freely, Freely" (Owens)
"O God, In Heaven" (Maquiso/Webb)

THE CALL TO WORSHIP
L: I bid you welcome from the cares and temptations of the world, to the worship of your Lord.

P: Be calm my soul, and take your ease away from the world.

L: Here you will learn of Christ Jesus, for he is the Way, the Truth, and the Life.

P: Learn well, my soul, that you may overcome, even as Christ overcame.

All: Now we are ready to worship God, and to receive nourishment for our souls.

CONGREGATIONAL PRAYER
Holy God, Father of our Lord Jesus Christ, we seek renewal and strength for our daily living. We would prepare ourselves to walk in the way of Jesus as we travel these days of Lent. Make us strong to face life's daily temptations. Forgive our sins, we pray, for we are often weak and succumb to temptations. Teach us to recognize those things within our lives

which displease you. Turn us around to follow your way, even as your son faithfully served you, in whose name we pray. Amen.

THE PASTORAL PRAYER

God of grace, love, and forgiveness, we, your children, are gathered to worship you. But we are mindful of our shortcomings and thus approach your throne asking for your mercy. We have not always placed you first, God; our own needs and wants seemed to get in the way. Sometimes the necessary duties of living prevented us from spending time with you. Sometimes we were having so much fun, we forgot about you; we forgot about your other children who do not have life as good as we do. More than anything we want to be better Christians. That's why we are here. More than anything we want to grow spiritually and follow the example of Jesus. That means we must live unselfishly; we must do deeds of kindness and mercy; we must honor you by the way we act and speak.

On this first Sunday of Lent, help us and walk with us as we follow Jesus. Help us to see that joy comes to those who serve you. In all the cares of life may we be aware of your blessings. In all the joys of life may we be aware of the needs of others.

(Here may follow intercessory prayers)

THE OFFERTORY PRAYER

We present these coins, bills, and checks to you for your blessing, Lord God. Work a miracle and change the coins and paper into deeds of love and mercy in accordance to your will, in Jesus' name. Amen.

THE BENEDICTION

Surely God sends his angels to guard you as you walk his way and obey his word. May you constantly be aware of God's love and mercy. May you receive grace that your spirit will grow during the season of Lent, even as Jesus overcame all temptation. Amen.

CHRIST: OUR EXAMPLE IN TEMPTATION

"I have set you an example that you should also do as I have done to you." John 13:15

Lectionary:

Genesis 2:15-17; 3:1-7	Temptation in Eden
Romans 5:12-19	Many made righteous through one
Matthew 4:1-11	Temptation of Jesus

Notes:
"A" — a disgruntled member of the congregation

"B" — the preacher

B: *(Reads the Scriptures for the day and begins to preach)* With such powerful Scripture lessons, I feel compelled to preach to you today about "Christ: Our Example in Temptation."

A: *(Seated in his pew, he calls out)* So! You're preaching about "Temptation" today! Seems to me that preachers are *always* harping about temptation. If you want us to avoid temptation, why not simply remove it?

B: If it could be as simple as that, God could have removed that certain tree from the Garden of Eden; you know, the "Tree of Knowledge of Good and Evil."

A: *(Stands on his feet)* Well, why didn't he? Isn't that where all the trouble began in the first place? Adam said: "Eve made me do it." Eve said: "The devil made me do it." And the devil (I suppose I should say "serpent") *could* have said: "God made me do it." He put the temptation there in the first place.

B: Obviously you believe that temptation is always someone else's fault.

A: *(Leaves his seat in congregation and walks up to the chancel to face the preacher)* Well, isn't it? Think about the story of Adam and Eve. Adam and Eve didn't accept any blame for their actions.

B: But that was the Old Testament reading. What about the temptation of Jesus, which we read from the Gospel of Matthew? I don't read where Jesus put the blame on anyone else.

A: All right; now that you've brought that up, I just don't see how that story is of any help to the ordinary guy walking down the street. I mean — turning stones to bread? Who's tempted to do that? We're tempted to *steal* the bread, or the money so we can buy the bread.

B: Granted. The story of Christ's temptation applies itself to a different example of behavior. This is not a matter of Jesus being tempted to petty thievery; this is a story of a real *power struggle*.

A: Are you telling me that Jesus was never tempted to steal?

B: I don't know the answer to that. After all, there is a large segment of his life's story that is unknown to us. Perhaps as a lad he may have experienced such a temptation. He was human, you know.

A: Okay. So it *is* possible Jesus experienced the common, ordinary variety of temptations. It's too bad these were never shared with us. Then maybe we could identify more closely with him.

B: You are forgetting something. All these so-called common, ordinary temptations *were* dealt with ages ago.

A: Oh? Explain yourself.

B: Case in point: The Ten Commandments! These deal with *all* the common sins of human beings.

A: Oh, yeah, I forgot about them. But they don't help *me* deal with temptation.

B: No, they tell us "don't!" If we *don't* do those things, then we actually overcome temptation.

A: Ha! I'd like to meet the person who actually never broke any of the rules!

B: Then you need to meet Jesus.

A: Here we go again. We've traveled round-robin, right back to my first premise. How does the story of the temptation of Jesus apply to my life and my temptations?

B: By demonstrating Jesus was superior in every way and was made our worthy leader and example.

A: I'm listening; go on.

B: As I indicated earlier, that encounter with Satan was a power struggle. Do you remember what happened just prior to the temptation story?

A: Let me think ... don't tell me ... I know! Jesus went into the wilderness and fasted for forty days. I guess he was a little hungry after that.

B: He probably was. But when he first began his wilderness experience, he was *searching for answers*. Up until that point in his life he lived as all other Jewish men (except he never married). He went to school, earned a living, and provided for his immediate family.

A: That's probably the period of his life when he experienced the *common* variety of temptation ... like the ones *we* deal with.

B: Again, probably. We only know that he was "the pure lamb of God, without spot or blemish," which tells us he overcame all the ordinary temptations.

A: And the ones in today's lesson were *ex*traordinary, right?

B: Definitely. I grant you that there *are* people who must deal with issues of power struggle, and these people could follow Christ's example ... for too many of them succumb to the lust for power. And as you have heard: "absolute power corrupts absolutely."

A: You sure are right there. When I stop to think about the way whole populations of people suffer, I wish *I* had the power to *take away* the power of corrupt leaders.

B: Then *you* would be the one that would have to deal with the temptation of power.

A: I guess I better be quiet and listen to what you have to say.

B: It was in the wilderness that Jesus wrestled with *who* he was, and *what* was expected of him as a result of who he was. How was he going to let the rest of the world know that he is the Messiah, the Son of God? Lots of men had tried the same thing: gathered a following around themselves, and tried to "take over" the Hebrew nation. All of them failed because none of them was the Son of God.

A: One would think that surely the Son of God could not fail! But in a way, he did fail.

B. Yes, in a way. But that comes up in a later period of his life, which also involved temptation.

A: Meanwhile, back in the desert ...

B: Back in the desert Jesus finally felt ready to end his fasting and begin his ministry. He probably had a plan worked out. This is where the temptations entered.

His human need of hunger brought on the first temptation. He could discover if he had any supernatural powers by turning stones into bread. That would surely prove, to himself at least, that he is the Son of God.

A: So? What would be so terrible about turning stones into bread? He was hungry. Even gods have a right to eat when they are hungry.

B: Ah! True! But remember that Jesus was sent to earth as a *human* so that he could experience all that humans experience. If he was going to use his powers to satisfy his every human need, how could he experience what we feel? He would never have to be hungry, or tired, or sick, or hurt. He would be divine, but not truly human.

A: I get it. The first temptation was a challenge to his humanness!

B: Because he overcame that temptation, we know that he would not use his divine nature to escape the pain of being human.

But there was still that temptation of wondering just how much power God had given to him. How could he find out?

A: That's when the devil told him to jump off the top of the temple. I sure would be afraid to try. What if it didn't work? I mean: Splat!

B: But what if it did? Then all those who saw this remarkable accomplishment would grovel at his feet and proclaim him as their leader!

A: Great! Then he would have had it made. The Messiahship was as good as his!

B: Except for one important factor. Jesus came to establish a kingdom of truth and love. These do not come about by spectacular feats of daring. Truth and love must start from the inside out. First Jesus had to win the hearts of the people. If people did not love him for who he was, they would only be superficial followers and would eventually become disenchanted.

A: Wasn't that third temptation a little unnecessary? Jesus proved his point. He proved he was superior to the devil.

B: Actually, the third temptation, once again, was a power struggle issue. Jesus could have done this "Messiah" thing the devil's way. Why go through a long, agonizing struggle to win the hearts of the people? He could assert his power from the start and take control of *all* the nations. That would be playing right into Satan's hands. Jesus knew that God the Father was really in control. All the kingdoms already belonged to God.

A: And what God really wants is for the people to love him with their hearts.

B: At last! You understand! Satan tried to get Jesus to set himself up as a world dictator. But Jesus didn't bite and the devil finally gave up.

A: You mentioned another temptation that came to him later on. Would you tell me about it?

B: Oh, yes ... we were speaking of the possibility of Jesus failing. This must have been on his mind when Judas betrayed him into the hands of the hostile leaders. Jesus knew this would happen, but he hoped it wouldn't. So he asked God for a different way out.

A: Who wouldn't! Death by crucifixion is not what anyone would choose!

B: That's the whole point. Jesus actually *chose* to die for us. The pure, unblemished Lamb of God became our sacrifice. He had the *power to avoid* going through the ignominy of apparent failure and actual suffering. *There* was the temptation — to use his divine power to avoid Calvary and rejection.

A: That was when he prayed in the Garden of Gethsemane: "Let this cup pass from me, but not my will; your will be done."

B: Very good. You show remarkable progress in your understanding. Yes, once again Jesus overcame temptation, the greatest temptation of all, and he consented to become our savior.

A: Thank God!

B: And thank you for having the courage to share your doubts with me and the congregation.

A: *(Takes his seat in the congregation)*

B: Let us pray:
    We thank you, God, for the example of Jesus, and how he taught us that we can overcome temptation. Help us to accept his kingdom of truth and love. Forgive us for the many times when we gave into temptation. We want the purity of Jesus to take over our lives so that we can live like him and follow his example. Amen.

SECOND SUNDAY IN LENT

Second Sunday In Lent Worship Helps

SCRIPTURES

Old Testament	Genesis 12:1-4a
New Testament	Romans 4:1-5, 13-17
Gospel	John 3:1-17
Psalter	Psalm 112

SUGGESTED HYMNS

"If Thou But Suffer God To Guide Thee" (Winkworth/ Neumark)

"Only Trust Him" (Stockton)

"Where He Leads Me" (Blandy/Norris)

"He Leadeth Me" (Gilmore/Bradbury)

"Of The Father's Love Begotten" (Divinum Mysterium)

THE CALL TO WORSHIP

L: Children of Abraham, come and worship the God who calls us to a new way.

P: We are children of The Way; who is Abraham?

L: He is the father of our faith, ancestor of all who believe in the true God.

P: We praise the God of Abraham. We praise the God of our fathers, for he is our God.

All: Let our song be heard; God is Lord of all and gladly we bring him our devotion and worship.

CONGREGATIONAL PRAYER

We have come apart from the world to worship you, God, for you have called us, and you alone are worthy of our praise. Almighty God, give us courage to walk in your holy way. Give us faith to venture into the unknown, satisfied to rely on your wisdom and grace. Where you lead us we will follow, for we know the world cannot give us the assurance of forgiveness and salvation. Forgive us when we stray from your path. Increase our faith in Jesus, in whose name we pray. Amen.

THE PASTORAL PRAYER

God of Abraham, of Israel, and all people, you call to each of us to forsake the old ways. Your Son challenges us to start life anew and to believe in him. The gospel is so clear, so simple, but we hesitate to let go of those things which give us pleasure for a brief while. All around us are people who capitalize on pleasure. They advertise, they market pleasures, and they get rich off our weaknesses and cravings. Give us courage to follow the truth. Forbid that we should follow after false promises. Jesus promised us eternal life, forgiveness, and inner peace. Jesus asked us to share the good news with everyone. Let this be our goal, because we know that there are those who have lost their way. Perhaps we can help lead them back to you. For those who are lost in a world of sin, we pray your mercy. For those who are ill, we pray your healing.

(Here may follow intercessory prayers)

THE OFFERTORY PRAYER

Because you are so generous, O God, we would not be stingy. Teach us the blessings that come through being generous, and grant that we may always give out of grateful hearts. Bless our offerings we pray in Jesus' name. Amen.

THE BENEDICTION

May God walk with you as you follow his way.
May you walk with God and not stray.
And may the forgiveness and peace of our blessed Lord
Be with you, always. Amen.

CHRIST, OUR EXAMPLE IN FAITH AND OBEDIENCE

Lectionary:
Genesis 12:1-4a   Abram called by God
Romans 4:1-5, 13-17   Faith makes us heirs with Abraham
John 3:1-17   Nicodemus' visit to Jesus

Notes:
"A" — press agent for Abraham — dressed like a sterotypical reporter, wearing hat with "press" written on a card and sticking out of the hatband for all to see

"B" — the preacher

B: Today we are going to consider the example which Jesus set for us as a person of faith and obedience. To help us understand today's scripture readings, I invited Abraham's press agent to meet with us today.
     Good morning!

A: Hey there! Glad to be here! In fact, it's great! One can never get too much publicity, you know. If it wasn't for you preachers and Sunday school teachers, most people wouldn't know about Abraham.

B: I suppose we could add another group to that list you just cited: Hebrew school students.

A: Oh, oh, you're right. I should never omit *them*. After all, Abraham was their ancestor!

B: That's interesting, especially in light of what Paul wrote to the Roman Christians. He said: "Abraham is the father of us *all*" (Romans 4:16b).

A: Well, there must be some mistake! Abraham was the ancestor of the *Jews*.

B: And the Moslems, don't forget.

A: Ahem. *(Clears throat and begins to squirm a little)* The Jews don't like to be reminded of Abraham's extra-curricular activities. They don't like to admit Ishmael was related to Abraham.

B: I bet they don't like to admit that we Christians are related to Abraham either.

A: Noooo, they *don't*. Abraham was a Jew.

B: That's where you are wrong. Abraham was not a Jew. His ancestry traces all the way back to Adam (Luke 3:23-38). Since Adam was the first man, that means we are *all* descendents of Adam and Abraham.

A: If Abraham wasn't a Jew, what was he, if you're so smart?

B: He was a Babylonian!

A: *(Groans)* How could you!? Maybe Abraham did live in Ur at one time of his life. The important thing is, *he moved out of that sin hole!*

B: Ahhh, now you're talking like a preacher instead of like a press agent. You have brought us up to the very area of my concern.

A: I have?

B: You just admitted Abraham moved away from a city of sin. What kind of sin?

A: Hmmm ... worshiping many gods?

B: Right. God wanted people to worship him as the True God. Where was he supposed to begin? He tried with Adam, but eventually Adam's descendents drifted away to other lands and forgot about the true God. Some biblical scholars believe the family of Abraham still worshiped one God and not idols. Perhaps that is why God decided to start all over again, so to speak, by choosing Abraham to start a whole new line of people. And Abraham was *obedient* to God's call.

A: Excuse me for interrupting, but didn't Abraham start a whole new nation — not just a new people? He started the *Hebrew* nation!

B: We are in agreement there. But let's move ahead two thousand years in history to the time of Jesus.

A: *(Interrupting)* Who *also* was a Jew!

B: Yes, *and* the Son of God, as well as a son of Abraham. *(Gives "A" an exasperated look and continues)* Well anyway, Jesus began his ministry by preaching good news to his countrymen ...

A: *(Interrupting again)* The Jews ... *(with a know-it-all look)*

B: *(Going on as if nothing happened)* ... and almost immediately Jesus became viewed as a threat to the religious leaders.

A: Why, if he was only preaching good news? Where's the threat in that?

B: Because the people were following after Jesus instead of the leaders, and the leaders were jealous and felt threatened.

A: Oh boy! If only I could have been his press agent! Look what I did for Abraham. All the *good* stuff written about him — that was *my* doing!

B: If I remember correctly, a few things in Abraham's record were not so favorable.

A: Well, you know how it is. You gotta keep readership interest up by adding a few spicy details. Heh, heh. *(Chuckles and gleefully rubs hands together)*

B: Maybe it's a good thing you *weren't* Jesus' press agent. Now, may I get on with my story?

A: Sure, go ahead!

B: Thank you. Because of the suspicion centered about Jesus, Nicodemus, one of those religious leaders I just mentioned, had a clandestine meeting with Jesus. He was interested in learning more about the teachings of Jesus, but he didn't want any of the other Pharisees to catch him talking to Jesus.

A: I still don't get it. Why would they have to meet *secretly*?

B: What you need to realize is that Jesus upset the neat money scam which was being operated at the temple. The ones who were hardest hit were the poor people. The scam was that no one could purchase a sacrificial animal with regular money, and, of course, most poor people did not own animals for sacrificing. They had to purchase them at the temple.

A: *(Acts astounded)* You're kidding!

B: No, it's true! All the people had to first go to a money changer so that their money could be exchanged for temple scrip. What it amounted to was the temple coffers were getting richer while the worshipers were getting cheated. After all, the leaders could set their own rate of exchange, and there was no one who could challenge them on it. They were a law unto themselves.

A: So what did Jesus do to upset the apple cart?

B: He did just that. He upset all the desks and tables of the money changers, spilling the money all over the place, and then he chased them out of the temple. After that he opened up the cages of the lambs and goats and doves and let them go free. He was really angry about the way the Pharisees were abusing God's house.

A: Whew! What a headline that would make: "Evangelist exposes temple money scam." Boy, do I wish I had been Jesus' press agent!

B: Apparently Jesus got enough publicity on his own. It forced Nicodemus to meet him secretly.

A: What *was* the result of that meeting, anyway?

B: I would say that Nick's life was changed. According to the records he continued to be a secret disciple of Jesus until *after* Jesus was put to death. Then he "came out of the closet," so to speak.

A: Back up a minute! Jesus was *put* to death? For exposing that temple money scam?

B: I guess that was part of it. But you need to concentrate a little more on what Jesus had to say to Nick that night.

A: Okay. Tell me.

B: Let's focus in on the sixteenth verse of John 3: "For God so loved the world that he gave his only begotten son, that whoever believes in him shall not perish but have everlasting life."

A: You weren't kidding when you said Jesus was the Son of God, were you?

B: No, I am in earnest. I see you picked up on a key phrase in that sentence — "God gave his only son." God gave Jesus to the world — to *everyone*, as a sacrificial lamb.

A: You mean like the little lambs that were killed on the altar at the temple whenever people sinned?

B: Precisely! Jesus was slaughtered, but *he laid* his *own* life on the altar — for the sins of whoever would believe in him. He didn't have to die; he was the son of God.

A: So why did he? Die, that is ...

B: Because God loved the whole world — everybody — and he wanted more than one nation ...

A: *(Interrupting)* You mean the Jews.

B: *(Nods and continues right on)* ... to serve him. He wanted *all* people to love him, not just the sons of Abraham. So Jesus was obedient to his father's will; "even unto death."

A: So that's how you Christians became heirs of Abraham — you did it through Jesus!

B: All those who have faith in God, who believe Jesus died for each one, and come to him for forgiveness, are forgiven of their sins.

A: That makes everyone a little bit like Abraham. We are *all*, each one of us, called to come away from our selfish lives and have faith to follow a "new way."

B: Look who's preaching now! Abraham is a great example of faith and obedience. He obeyed God and trusted God's promise to make "of him a great nation."

A: *(Interrupting again)* Even though he had no kids. Ooops! I mean children.

B: Thank you. You took the words out of my mouth. God eventually did give Abraham an heir, and from Isaac descended the great Hebrew nation ...

A: But you are supposed to tell us about the example of *Jesus* in faith and obedience.

B: Do all press agents make it their business to be so disruptive? I'm leading up to that.
      On the other hand, Jesus was called out of heaven to fulfill a purpose on earth. In every way Jesus was faithful and obedient:
      His faith and obedience to his heavenly father was unswerving.
      His faith in his followers continued, even when they forsook him at his trial. That faith eventually paid off.
      And, he had faith in himself and his ultimate goal — to spread the good news of God's love and to win the battle over sin and death.

A: You know, you'd make a pretty decent press agent. I'm glad I met you. I only wish that I had met Jesus. *(He shakes hands with "B" and begins to walk away)*

B: *(Calls after "A" as he leaves)* There's no reason you can't meet Jesus. All you need is faith to believe in him, and obedience to follow his way.
      Let us pray: God of love and mercy, increase our faith in you and the redemptive act of Jesus. Help us to be faithful and obedient to your will for our lives. Amen.

THIRD SUNDAY IN LENT

Third Sunday In Lent Worship Helps

SCRIPTURES

Old Testament	Exodus 17:1-7
New Testament	Romans 5:1-11
Gospel	John 4:5-42
Psalter	Psalm 95:1-11

SUGGESTED HYMNS

"Fill My Cup, Lord" (Blanchard)

"Come, Thou Fount" (Robinson/Wyeth)

"Rock Of Ages" (Toplady/Hastings)

"Lord, Speak To Me" (Havergal/Schumann)

"Let My People Seek" (O'Driscoll/Williams)

THE CALL TO WORSHIP

L: Welcome to this place where we worship the true God.

P: We are glad to be here, but is this the only place where we may worship God?

L: God is a Spirit; those who would worship God must worship him in Spirit and Truth.

P: So, to truly worship God, our hearts must become God's altar.

All: Our spirits will worship God in truth, grateful we can worship God, no matter where we may be.

CONGREGATIONAL PRAYER

God almighty, when we were in the wilderness of confusion and sin, we needed a leader to save us, so you sent your son. Jesus willingly went into the wilderness and experienced hunger and thirst. So when our souls are thirsty he will fill us with living water. When our lives are empty, he will nourish us and cause us to be strong. We come away from the noise and busy-ness of the struggle with life to the quietness of worship, longing to be filled. Feed us, we pray, that we will have

strength to rise above those things which cause us to lose faith in you. Live in and through us, for Jesus' sake. Amen.

THE PASTORAL PRAYER

This is the third week of our Lenten journey, O God, and some of us seem to be caught in a valley of confusion. We began strong of purpose, resolved to grow into a deeper understanding of you and ourselves. Now we seem to be lost in a wilderness; our thirst increases, but we know it not. Strike the rock of our indifference, our spiritual apathy, and allow your spirit to mingle with our spirits until we are aware of only this precious moment of fellowship with you, of our spirits intertwined. Then we can become of one purpose, living out your ideal for our lives, and for your kingdom.

We praise you for the gift of faith, faith that gives us courage to walk with Jesus all the way to Calvary. It was at Calvary that life flowed as freely as water over rocks, flooding down through the ages to touch every soul who seeks salvation.

We praise you for the ordinary joys of life which help make our lives extraordinary. And we humbly intercede in behalf of those who have special needs ...

(Here may follow intercessory prayers)

THE OFFERTORY PRAYER

If you would bless these small offerings, O God, they could flow like a mighty river to touch and bless the lives of those in need of your touch through us. We give these gifts to you, in Jesus' name. Amen.

THE BENEDICTION

Be happy that God knows all about you, yet still loves you. Share this good news with others that they may be happy, too, through the mercy of Jesus who fills you with his living water. Amen.

CHRIST: OUR EXAMPLE IN LOVE

Lectionary:
> Exodus 17:1-7   Water from the rock
> Romans 5:1-11   At the right time, Christ died for sinners
> John 4:5-24   Woman at the well

Notes:
"A" — a Samaritan (man) from the city of Sychar. May be costumed if so desired

"B" — the preacher

B: *(Reads John 4:5-42, then announces to the congregation)* Today I have invited a special guest to help me with the sermon. His name is Arad, and he is a Samaritan citizen from the city of Sychar. I trust you will extend to Arad your courteous attention.

Good morning, Arad.

A: Good morning, Pastor. Thank you for the invitation to address your congregation. I am a bit nervous; I've never done anything like this.

B: Arad, you heard our Gospel lesson read a few minutes ago. Because you were a witness at this event, it is my hope that you will be able to shed a little more light on what happened that day.

A: To be honest, I was a witness to only the second part of the story. I did not actually see Jesus and Myra at the beginning of the story, although I have always known Myra. I'm truly pleased to hear the Gospel account of the story, because that means Myra was really telling the truth from the start.

B: You had doubts about what Myra told you?

A: Initially I did. Myra's reputation left a little to be desired, you know.

B: Yes, the story account does allude to some of Myra's past, especially the fact that she was (quote) "living with a man out of wedlock."

A: Oh, I don't wish to condemn the woman. Probably most of the gossip was untrue. You know how stories have a way of getting out of hand in a small town.

B: Did you have a personal relationship with Myra?

A: I knew Myra quite well. In fact, I knew *all* the townsfolk. I was Myra's physician.

B: Then I should have introduced you as *Doctor* Arad. I beg your pardon for the omission. We would really like to hear something of Myra's life before she met Jesus.

A: She was really a victim of circumstances, you know. Myra grew up in a middle-class family, the only girl among four brothers. When she turned fourteen, her parents found her a husband. But unlike most young women, Myra was not ready for marriage, especially with the older man her parents selected as her groom.

B: We tend to forget that such marriages were arranged for Middle Eastern girls. We also forget how young they were when they married.

A: Myra was at the right age. She could bear children, she had a dowry, and she could have a very secure future as the wife of a respected townsman.

B: But according to the Gospel, Myra had five husbands.

A: That is correct. Her first husband lived only a few months following their marriage, and since she was without child, the law stated that the groom's brother had to take Myra as a wife and raise up an heir. Unfortunately for Myra, her first husband came from a large family, and all his brothers were older than he.

B: I get the picture. Myra was given from one older man to another in marriage, then to the next, each time one of the husbands died.

A: Right. By the time Myra was 25 years old, she had been married — and widowed — five times! And still there were no children as the result of those marriages.

B: As a woman, my heart goes out to her. To be widowed so many times, at such a young age!

A: The saddest part of Myra's story is her complete unhappiness. She resented every marriage because she rebelled against the custom of pre-arranged marriage. As the only girl among four brothers, Myra was doted upon by her brothers. She became somewhat of a tomboy, joining in with their games and helping with their chores. She determined in her heart she wanted a husband who would be as handsome and kind and lively as her brothers.

B: And her marriages gave her none of these aspirations?

A: No, and as a result she became moody and depressed. I tried to help her through this period of her life, but she had a strong aversion to "older men," avoiding them as if they had the plague. To Myra, I was an "older" man.

B: So, did she turn to the women of the town for friendship?

A: Oh, no! She was considered an outcast. All those marriages and no children!

B: The poor thing. No husbands, no friends. What did she do?

A: She began to hang out at the local tavern where she could enjoy male companionship like she used to have with her brothers when she was a child.

B: It is always a sad thing when people seek companionship at such places instead of going to a church where they could meet people who would be more helpful.

A: You are forgetting that we Samaritans did not have churches, per se. The religious of our community were looking toward to the day when a deliverer would come. Then they could worship freely without condemnation by the Jews.

B: You are right. As a result, the Samaritan people fell away from the worship of God, causing further ostracizing from the Jewish people ... even though both nations descended from the same Jewish ancestors.

A: Myra made many friends — all of them men — and eventually lived as a common-law wife with one to whom she was especially attracted.

B: So she was apparently performing her "wifely" duty of getting water for the household on the day she met Jesus.

A: Yes, but notice she did not go to the well at the time when the women of the town went to draw water. She was all alone at the well ...

B: ... still unaccepted by the women of the town, so she avoided them. I find it interesting that Myra had her defenses in place when Jesus spoke to her.

A: She may have been a "liberated" woman, but she was first of all a Samaritan. Jesus was a man, but he was a Jew. Yes, she was defensive when it came to Jews.

B: Because he was a compassionate man, Jesus eventually won her trust. He knew exactly how to draw her out of herself. The fact that he seemed to accept her in spite of her lifestyle was the clincher, so to speak. He had a way of tying the ordinary areas of life with the spiritual areas.

Water became a symbol for eternal life.

Thirst became a longing for spiritual truths.

The truth about her living with a man became a touchstone for the greater truth about the nature of God.

A: Myra was so excited about meeting the Messiah she forgot all about her water jar. Instead she ran back to town to tell the people what had happened.

"Why should we listen to you?" asked one of the wives. "You are only a tramp!"

"That's just it!" Myra joyously replied. "He knows all about my past, and still he spoke to me. How could he know about me? He must be the Messiah!"

B: Wow! Myra was willing to risk further shame and rejection in order to tell the people about Jesus! She was telling the good news of the Gospel — that God accepts us, where we are. If we would only be honest and confess our sins, God's mercy and love would pour forgiveness into our lives.

So tell me, Doctor Arad, how did Myra finally convince the townsfolk to go see Jesus?

A: Actually, her male companions from the local tavern were the first to believe her. They knew Myra was basically a good woman and they were impressed with her story. So once a few people became excited, the energy spread and many people went to meet the man at the well. They were so impressed that they invited Jesus to stay in their town for a few days.

B: Doctor, I certainly appreciate your contribution to our service ...

A: *(Interrupting)* There's still one more thing you need to hear.

B: Oh? Very well, share it with me.

A: You know, of course, that the Jews and Samaritans are hostile toward one another. In fact, they *despise* one another, me included. After I met Jesus and felt his love, my life changed also. The change that came over me was remarkable; I no longer hated people — not even the Jews. Because of the love of Jesus, I was able to help a Jew who had been left to die along the road by some robbers. I dressed his wounds and even took him to an inn so that he could receive further care, and I paid for it!

    Before the love of Jesus came into my life, I *never* would have helped a Jew, even though I am a physician.

B: Doctor, I'm so glad you shared the rest of your story with me! Jesus' love made a difference in the lives of you and Myra and your townsfolk. Nearly 2,000 years have passed and Jesus' love is still making a difference in the lives of people. The result? We love — because he first loved us!

    Let us pray:

    Help us, Lord God, to be as open and receptive to Jesus as were those Samaritan townsfolk. Because of your love and acceptance of us, may we, in turn, follow this example and accept others with love and acceptance, in the name of Jesus. Amen.

FOURTH SUNDAY IN LENT

Fourth Sunday In Lent Worship Helps

SCRIPTURES

Old Testament	1 Samuel 16:1-13
New Testament	Ephesians 5:8-14
Gospel	John 9:1-41
Psalter	Psalm 23

SUGGESTED HYMNS

"Heal Me, Hands Of Jesus" (Perry/Warren)
"I Want To Walk As A Child Of The Light" (Thomerson)
"The Lord's My Shepherd" (Irvine/Crimond)
"Savior, Like A Shepherd" (Thrupp/Bradbury)
"Open My Eyes" (Scott)
"O Zion, Haste" (Thomson/Walch)

THE CALL TO WORSHIP

L: Today we worship a loving Shepherd who welcomes us into the safety of the fold.

P: "All we like sheep have gone astray; we have wandered each to our own way."

L: Today we also worship Jesus, our gentle healer.

P: "Heal me, hands of Jesus" ... open my eyes, cleanse my heart, and renew my energy.

All: Our Healing Lord and Loving Shepherd, we thank you for accepting our worship and for accepting us. Amen.

CONGREGATIONAL PRAYER (especially intended for "One Great Hour of Sharing")

Father God, giver of all good gifts, we bow before you as needy persons. We are in need of mercy and forgiveness. We are in need of a shepherd to lead us. We are in need of spiritual sight and understanding. Yet, in the midst of our need we are aware of others who have great needs, for this is the day we share our resources. As we give to the needs of others, may we

be always mindful of your tender mercies to us, and be determined to walk in the light of your love and instruction, taught to us by Jesus, your Son, in whose name we pray. Amen.

THE PASTORAL PRAYER

Creator God, by whom nature herself exists, our own natures are attuned to the changes of the seasons. To those who are sensitive, the subtle indications of spring's arrival stirs light and optimism within. The long nights of winter, the depression of cold and grayness will slowly melt and trickle into warmth and hope. Just as our nature bids us awaken to the season of spring, so we pray that your spirit will awaken us to your grace and warmth.

We would be sensitive to your purity so that our lives may be filled with goodness.

We would be sensitive to your goodness so that our lives may reflect kindness.

On this day we make a special effort to share a little extra of our resources. On this day we unite with churches all around to give a little extra to those with special needs as we observe the "One Great Hour of Sharing." Let this truly be a great hour, an hour when we become renewed, spiritually fed, and responsive to the challenge to serve others.

We lift the needs of your children, praying for the hungry, the oppressed, the estranged and the lost, the sick and the dying.

(Here may follow intercessory prayers)

THE OFFERTORY PRAYER

Our eyes, ears and hearts are open to your touch and your bidding, Lord. You bid us give that others may live. Accept our gifts and bless them. May our eyes and hearts continue to be sensitive to the needs of your children, in Jesus' name. Amen.

THE BENEDICTION

We have sung together, prayed together, and fellowshiped with one another. In the beauty of this fellowship, may you go forth as God's people to a world of physical and spiritual need, spreading his good news wherever you go. Amen.

CHRIST: OUR EXAMPLE IN MEEKNESS AND STRENGTH

Lectionary:

1 Samuel 16:1-13	Anointing of David
Ephesians 5:8-14	Live as children of the Light
John 9:1-41	Healing of the blind man

Notes:
"A" — a lawyer (could be male or female)

"B" — the preacher

B: *(Reads John 9:1-41, then announces to congregation)* Our guest today is a lawyer from the city of Jerusalem. His (her) name is Tabia, and he (she) learned of this case secondhand.

A: That is correct. It so happened that I was at court that day and I missed all the excitement.

B: Tell me, Tabia, are you a secular lawyer, or do you restrict your practice to religious matters?

A: Actually, I accept secular and religious cases, although the Jews never really separate religion and state. No matter what the crime, it always broke one of the religious laws. Let's take today's story as an example of what I mean. If Jesus and the blind man had been Roman citizens, the matter would have ended after he had been healed. But the Jews had to make a big deal of it because they claimed Jesus broke the law.

B: Before we discuss what Jesus did, suppose we talk about what he had to say to his disciples. As you remember, they wanted to know for whose sins the man was being punished: his own, or his parents. This would infer that every blind person was blind because of his sin or his ancestor's sin.

A: What an unforgiving lot of people they were! They never forgave the sins or errors of people, even after they died! Consequently a blind person was not trained to live with his handicap; he was a sinner and was forced to live as a beggar.

B: Then along comes Jesus, who taught that God can be revealed even in a man born blind. As if to prove his point, he proceeds to heal the man in question.

A: *That's* when Jesus committed his sin! When he made that mud-pack for the man's eyes, he performed a task that is reserved for the pottery industry, and when you do the work of a potter, you break the law that commands no work to be done on the Sabbath!

B: But isn't that a little ridiculous? I would call that stretching the point, gross overexaggeration!

A: You are right, of course. But that, and his other error, was enough to add fuel to the fire.

B: What other error?

A: Telling the blind man to go and wash. That, too, was a Sabbath "no-no."

B: Well, if Jesus was the one who broke the Sabbath law, how is it that the Pharisees brought in the innocent man — the blind man — for questioning?

A: From what I've heard, it was because the religious leaders were afraid to have Jesus arrested on some trumped-up charge. They knew how much the public admired the man, and they were afraid of pressure from the people.

B: So they caught the smaller fish — probably hoping to use it as bait to catch their larger trophy. Tell me, Tahia, if you had been called in on the case, whose side would you defend? The Pharisees? Or the blind man? Or Jesus?

A: If I were practicing law in your century, I would be known as a "criminal" lawyer. I chose to defend those who wanted to fight the system. I enjoyed finding loopholes and meeting the challenge of arguing against their petty regulations. So I would have defended the blind man and his healer.

B: Do you think it was fair for the Pharisees to subpoena the man's parents?

A: Even the neighbors were in disagreement about the miracle. Apparently that act of washing turned a dirty beggar into a respectable man. He was so changed that they couldn't be certain he was really the same man.

B: What a beautiful insight! That's exactly what happens when Jesus cleanses someone of his sins! When people are washed in the waters of baptism and cleansed with his sacrificial blood, they are changed — they become new people!

A: I'm sure I don't know what you're talking about, but I'm glad I was able to touch on some philosophy that pleased you.

B: So since the neighbors couldn't testify on his behalf, the authorities decided to bring in his parents. They testified that he was indeed their son, but they wouldn't talk about how he was healed. Their courage took them only so far.

A: Now there's where the court was wrong. They had no right to excommunicate people because of their belief about the man Jesus. But those poor people didn't know that; they were scared and pushed any further witnessing onto their son.

B: So they bring back to the witness stand the man who had been blind.

A: I'll say this for that man: he had courage and he had intelligence. Not only did he stand up for his rights, he had the audacity to challenge the spirituality of the religious leaders!

B: I think that if I had been in that courtroom I would have been tempted to applaud his testimony.

A: Since he had no one to defend him, that man was excommunicated from the synagogue. Those leaders became so angry with the man's witness that they threw him out. They drove him out even though he didn't do anything wrong. I could have helped that man. I could have won an acquittal for him.

B: It's too bad he didn't know about you — but then he probably couldn't have afforded you. He was a beggar and didn't have much money.

A: True. My fees are a little steep.

B: Okay. Let's review what has happened so far. 1. Jesus heals a blind man, so that others may see that God can work through anyone. 2. The townsfolk take the healed man to the Pharisees.

A: Yes, that's the general procedure when people are healed. They must prove it to the Pharisees so that they can be declared "ritually clean."

B: 3. The Pharisees accuse Jesus of being a sinner because he "worked" on the Sabbath. 4. The Pharisees refuse to believe that a sinner could perform the miracle of healing a blind man. 5. They hold a hearing and summon the blind man — not just once, but twice, to testify. 6. They throw out all the evidence of the witnesses and excommunicate the man.

A: But the story doesn't end there. There is still the matter of the man called Jesus.

B: You're right. Word of what happened reached Jesus, so he decided to go find the blind man — I mean the man who had been blind. (He was never given a name.)

A: That speaks very highly for your Jesus. After all, he knew that the authorities were out to get him, but he didn't back off. I wonder if he imparted some of his courage to the blind man when he healed him?

B: That's a good point. When Jesus heals people, it's as though they receive some of the very nature of Jesus into their lives. If I didn't believe that, I wouldn't stand in this pulpit and preach that Jesus is the Son of God.

A: Obviously, by his own witness, the blind man believed that Jesus was from God. I'm surprised that others were not equally convinced. Yet, if this Jesus was really the Messiah, he would have cleaned up that mess of religious leaders and brought about a change, a revolution!

B: That was not his way. Change and revolution came about person-by-person. When the individual meets Jesus with simple faith (I should say "simple *blind* faith") his life is changed. Christianity has been working that way for the past 2000 years ... Jesus changing the individual.

A: For my part, I think he could have done a lot more good by cleaning up the system than to heal just one blind man.

B: He tried to change the system by changing the Pharisees, but unless the individial was changed in his own heart, really changed, the system would never change, especially by force.

A: So that's why Jesus told the Pharisees that they were the ones who were blind.

B: Their blindness was self-imposed. They knew the truth, and that made their sin all the worse.

A: The more I reflect on this story, the more I come to realize that Jesus was truly very strong. It takes a great deal of courage to stand up to the religious authorities, and that's what he did. He never backed off for a minute.

B: Even when he had to stand at his own trial, Jesus never backed off. A weaker person (such as you or I) would have succumbed to the pressure and tried to save himself. But not Jesus. He allowed the authorities to execute him.

A: But why? That's so senseless! What good can a dead man do?

B: If you would believe that Jesus is the Son of God, you would know that Jesus is not a "dead man." His story goes beyond his execution, for we believe that Jesus conquered death and lives with God, his Father.

A: I've heard rumors to that effect. But I find such a thing very difficult to believe. After all, I'm a lawyer, and I base most of my cases on fact, not rumor.

B: That's where the theory of working with the individual comes into play. If you would allow Jesus to heal your blindness, you would come to know that his strength is now your strength. His victory over death becomes your assurance of eternal life. His sacrificial death becomes your means of salvation from sin. And when you become changed, you can be the means for another person to become changed.

A: I begin to understand. Change cannot be forced on a person, nor can it be truly forced upon a nation ... no more than the Romans could force the Jews to become Roman citizens. In their hearts they would always be Jews.

B: The strength of Jesus was his meekness, his willingness to endure all so that we may be healed of our blindness and become changed creatures.

Let us pray:
Lord God, give us the determination to be healed through the touch of Jesus, so that we no longer surrender ourselves blindly to sin. As forgiven people, let us follow the way of Jesus and bring others for healing. Amen.

FIFTH SUNDAY IN LENT

Fifth Sunday In Lent Worship Helps

SCRIPTURES

Old Testament	Ezekiel 37:1-14	
New Testament	Romans 8:6-11	
Gospel	John 11:1-45	
Psalter	Psalm 130	

SUGGESTED HYMNS

"There Is A Balm in Gilead" (Spiritual)
"Crown Him With Many Crowns" (Bridges/Elvey)
"Easter People, Raise Your Voices" (James/Smart)
"Come, Ye Disconsolate" (Moore/Webbe)
"God Of Grace And God Of Glory" (Fosdick/Hughes)

THE CALL TO WORSHIP

L: Enter into the worship of our Resurrected Lord, for he lives and dwells with us.

P: We are still walking the Lenten path to Calvary, yet you speak of resurrection?

L: While on the way to Calvary, Christ conquered death; he raised Lazarus from the tomb.

P: Our Lord had such great power, and yet he willingly died for our sins!

All: Through our baptism we die to sin and rise to new life in Christ Jesus, all because of Calvary and Easter. Thanks be to God!

CONGREGATIONAL PRAYER

God of the living, we adore you because you are pure and holy. We, too, would be holy and forsake the valley of sin and death. Restore new life to our dry bones of contention and strife. Breathe your spirit of life into our feebleness until we become living models of your image, filled with your grace and love. Help us to move from our tombs of selfishness to share

new life with others who are spiritually dead. For Jesus' sake, hear our prayer. Amen.

THE PASTORAL PRAYER

Ever-living God, your spirit breathed life into a universe and gave it soul. Your spirit breathed soul into the body of a creature and gave him life. Your spirit breathed life into a people and gave them purpose. Through the ages your spirit has guided and prompted your people to bring the good news of your creative love to those whose souls are dying. What good is life if the soul is dead? We are like the dry bones of Ezekiel's vision; breathe new life into us again. Let us rise, clean and new and full of your spirit. Then, as spirit-filled creatures we will be empowered to share this new life. There are millions who do not know you. Help us to have a vision of how their lives could be changed, just as we were made new creatures in Christ.

Thank you for coming to us this day. Thank you for all your mercies. Thank you for answered prayer. Now hear our intercessory prayers as we continue ...

(Here may follow intercessory prayers)

THE OFFERTORY PRAYER

O Great Giver, power and strength to gain wealth came from you. Forgiveness and new life comes from you. We acknowledge all that we have and all that we are comes from your hand. Therefore we have brought you a gift to show our gratitude, a small token of our love. We offer our gift to you for your blessing, in Jesus' name. Amen.

THE BENEDICTION

Once again you have been fed and your spirits renewed. On this Sabbath day, take your enjoyment and go home to reflect on the gracious words you have heard. May the inspiration of God's Holy Spirit continue to guide you through this week of activity as you follow the way of Christ. Amen.

Fifth Sunday In Lent Dialogue

CHRIST: OUR EXAMPLE IN POWER AND DEED

Lectionary:
>   Ezekiel 37:1-14   Valley of the Dry Bones
>   Romans 8:6-11   New life through the Spirit
>   John 11:1-45   Raising of Lazarus

Notes:
"A" — Lazarus

"B" — the preacher

B: *(Reads John 11:1-45, then announces to congregation)* Because so many people long to speak with someone from the dead, spiritualists continue to intrigue us with their seances. I have arranged for someone to visit us from the dead — but not by a seance. This is a hypothetical situation. We just heard the story of Lazarus, so now let us meet Lazarus.

Good morning, Lazarus.

A: Good morning. I'm not so certain I am glad to be here. Did you know that you are the third pastor this week that has bothered me?

B: *(Apologetically)* I beg your forgiveness. I didn't realize I was bothering you. Were you doing something important?

A: Well, I guess so! We were all preparing for the annual celebration known as "The Festival of Bethany."

B: Oh, so you observe celebrations in the Land of the Living. I guess I never thought about what you all do once you leave us. Could you tell us a little about the Festival of Bethany?

A: Hey, Man (Ma'am)! The Land of the Living is a happy place. We don't just sit around and twiddle our thumbs. We get into the spirit of the occasion, and believe me, there are plenty of occasions! Take the Festival of Bethany, for example. So much happened at Bethany that a bunch of us got together to petition Peter (you know who he is, don't you?) to see if we could officially celebrate Bethany.

B: I would think you would have a Festival of Jerusalem as opposed to Bethany.

A: Oh, we do have a Festival of Jerusalem, and of Bethlehem, and Plymouth Rock, and Harlem, and Johannesburg and ... *(gets interrupted)*

B: Oh, good grief! You probably don't have enough days to observe all your celebrations. Sounds to me like all you do is play.

A: As I said: "The Land of the Living is a happy place. We don't just ...

A & B: "... sit around and twiddle our thumbs!"

B: Okay. Now tell me about Bethany.

A: For one thing, Bethany was where the parade *began* when Jesus made his triumphal entry into Jerusalem. It was there that Simon the Leper gave a feast for Jesus and where Jesus' feet were anointed. It's close to the Garden of Gethsemane. And, most importantly, Bethany was *my* hometown.

B: That's right. You, Mary, and Martha lived there and Jesus used to stay there on occasions.

A: Don't forget — it was the site of the most amazing miracle which Jesus ever performed — bringing me back to life *after* I had been buried for four days.

B: Ah. *Now* we're getting to the topic of my special interest. I wonder if you could tell me a few things. When people — modern-day people, that is — die, and then come back to life again, many of them say they saw a bright light and felt a tremendous peace. Did you see a bright light when you died?

A: Nope. I've been asked that question again and again. I didn't see a thing. I was sick one moment, and then — nothing! That is, until I had to struggle with those stupid grave clothes.

B: Interesting. Now explain about the grave clothes.

A: Well, the first thing you did to a dead person was to wrap him up, like a mummy. My head, my arms, my legs, my feet ... they were all wrapped up tight with linen cloths. Jesus had some sense of humor, expecting me to "arise and come forth" when I couldn't even walk. I had to hop up the steps, and that wasn't easy because I could hardly bend my legs.

B: That explains why Jesus commanded them to "unbind you."

A: You should have heard the screams when I finally got out of the tomb. I couldn't see anything, but men and women were screaming — like they had seen a ghost.

B: Can you imagine the trauma of your sisters? You were buried for four days; they held your funeral; they were in mourning; and then, Pow! You're alive!

A: When I finally understood what had happened, I also was in a state of shock. Mary and Martha made a big show of their affection, but they always were emotional. You'd think I was a hero — all I did was die. Jesus was the hero; he performed the miracle! So our Festival of Bethany is really in honor of Jesus and all that he did when he was in Bethany.

B: Just as you give honor to Jesus for the miracle, Jesus gave honor to his Father God. He made certain that the crowd heard his prayer to God. Jesus wanted so much to have the people believe that he came from God, that his power came from God.

A: I'll tell you this: my sisters and I believed he came from God, especially after he brought me back to life. I mean, we believed he was the Messiah before that happened, but that miracle helped us to believe in the resurrection. Nobody was really sure about the hereafter.

B: According to the gospel acount, many other people believed in Jesus because of what he had done. But apparently there were some who must have thought it to be a trick, for they went running to the authorities to tell them about the miracle.

A: Those were *bad* times. The high priest prophesied that one man must die for the good of all, so from that day onward, they planned on how they could kill Jesus. Jesus had to go into hiding with his disciples.

B: If only the religious leaders could have believed Jesus came from God — just imagine how different history would have been! If only they hadn't seen his power as a threat. The most wonderful thing of all was that Jesus never used his power in a selfish way, or in a way that would hurt anyone.

A: True; but when men are selfish and hunger after power for themselves, they see all other power as a threat. Even the good deeds of Jesus could not persuade them otherwise. I hoped that after a while things would kind of die down so that Jesus could come out into the open again.

B: How long did Jesus stay undercover?

A: Actually it was only a few months. The Passover festival was at hand, and Jesus was determined to come to Jerusalem with all the other pilgrims. Naturally he stayed at my home since Bethany is only two miles from Jerusalem, about a half-hour walk, all downhill.

B: At least he was safe at your house.

A: Not really. When the townsfolk found out that Jesus and his twelve disciples were staying at my house, the word quickly spread, not just in Bethany, but all the way to Jerusalem.

B: I remember reading about that dinner at your house. Mary anointed Jesus' feet with expensive perfume. Judas felt that she could have washed his feet with water — like everyone else. He would have sold the perfume and used the money for himself.

A: Ah, yes. Mary had a flamboyant side to her. Besides, nothing was too good for the man who brought me back to life. But the real reason she loved him so much was that he turned her around from a life of sin. Mary became a different woman after Jesus came into her life. For that matter, all of us became different because Jesus came into our lives.

B: Lazarus, that is still happening two thousand years later. Jesus continues to change the lives of people who come to him. The effect of his power tranverses time and oceans.
    But I'm curious. How did the rumor get all the way to Jerusalem that Jesus was back in Bethany?

A: You know how it is with rumors. Who knows how they get started? All I know is that people came to Bethany in droves! They had two reasons for coming: they wanted to see Jesus, of course; and then they wanted to see the man who had been raised from the dead. I felt like someone on exhibit!

B: I guess you were a celebrity, at that.

A: Yeah, but there wasn't much endearing about the experience. Not only were the authorities out to destroy Jesus, they put out an all-points bulletin on *my* head as well. "Wanted! Dead!" — not alive!

B: Apparently you were both a threat to their political power over the people. They recognized that Jesus had power, and now that you came back from the grave, they probably were afraid that you also had similar power.

A: That's what I find so remarkable about the whole situation. Sure, Jesus had power. But he always used his power for good: to heal the sick, feed the hungry, forgive sins. Why would anyone be threatened by that power?

B: Only evil needs to fear the power of Jesus Christ. Jesus conquered sin, and he conquered death, the consequence of sin. Those religious leaders were selfish and did not want to lose hold of the power they held over the people. If they truly had loved God, they would have loved the people and would have wanted what was best for them.

A: What hurts most is to realize that all those people who went with us into Jerusalem the day Jesus made his triumphant entry into that city suddenly cringed under the power of the authorities. When the chips were down, they disappeared into the stones of the city.

B: It must be that they had not experienced for themselves the forgiving power of Jesus.

A: You are right. All those followers of Jesus dwindled down to a small minority of persons — and these were people who had their lives changed as a result of his power in them.

B: Lazarus, when you return to Mary and Martha, tell them that the power of Jesus Christ is still at work in the world today. It works in the lives of those people who turn to him for forgiveness and pledge their lives to him. The Calvary experience did not end the power of our Lord, it enhanced it. But then, you knew that.

A: Pastor, thank you for this opportunity to talk. But my beeper is ringing again, and I have a feeling that another church and its pastor wants an interview. Whew! Lent is a busy season for me. So long. Shalom. Peace!

B: Peace to you, my friend. We'll meet again through the power of our Lord.

Let us pray:
Lord, visit us again with your power. We want the assurance that we will live with you in the resurrection. We want the assurance that in our lives here on earth, we may live with you in purity of heart. As a result of your power living in us, help us to be powerful influences in this world of sin so that others may come to know your love and forgiveness. Amen.

SIXTH SUNDAY IN LENT

(PALM/PASSION SUNDAY)

Sixth Sunday In Lent Worship Helps
(Palm/Passion Sunday)

SCRIPTURES

Palm Sunday reading	Matthew 21:1-11
Psalter	Psalm 118:14-29
Passion Sunday reading	Isaiah 50:4-9a
	Philippians 2:5-11

SUGGESTED HYMNS

Palm Sunday Hymns

"Hosanna, Loud Hosanna" (Threlfall/Monk)

"Tell Me The Stories Of Jesus" (Parker/Challinor)

"There's Something About That Name" (Gaither)

Passion Sunday Hymns

"What Wondrous Love Is This" (Christiansen)

"O Sacred Head, Now Wounded" (Passion Chorale)

"Ah, Holy Jesus" (Heerman/Cruger)

THE CALL TO WORSHIP

L: This is a day of two celebrations: one is happy, while the other is a grim reminder.

P: "Joy and sorrow are two sides of the same coin," so let our joy be tempered by our sadness.

L: And let your sadness be turned to joy, for the road to Calvary led to the empty tomb.

P: Thank you for reminding us.

All: We will walk this holy week with Christ, confident in the glorious outcome. Let our worship prepare us for both aspects.

CONGREGATIONAL PRAYER

Holy God, gladly do we proclaim your son as our Lord and King. We wish that all the world could join us in this exaltation. Our hearts are saddened to realize that Jesus and his Way are continually rejected by those he came to save. Through your grace, God, keep us faithful to our allegiance which we

pledged to Christ when first we followed him. Give us the strength to walk with Jesus along the dark road to Golgotha, and to remain at his side until the conclusion. Grant that we may share in Christ's final triumph, even the victory over sin and death. Amen.

THE PASTORAL PRAYER

Father God, on this special Sunday we contemplate with marvel and respect the courage of your son. He went to Jerusalem to die; that is sad. Worse than that! He went to Jerusalem to be rejected! His life's work for naught!

God, you know that the fear of rejection is a constant factor in our lives. Your children do stupid things just to become accepted by family, peers, and those in authority. The fear of being rejected by you should be our first concern. But that's why Jesus came to earth, not simply to die, but to provide a way for us to be acceptable in your sight.

We believe in the cause of Jesus, so we follow him in triumph. We believe in the mediation of Jesus, so we follow him to Calvary. We believe in the power of Jesus, for we experience the forgiveness of sin and we receive new life. Thank you, God, for the faithful obedience of your son. May he be Lord of our lives.

Thank you for our daily gifts and blessings ...

(Here may follow intercessory prayers)

THE OFFERTORY PRAYER

Our Gracious God, we cannot strew our garments for Christ to walk upon, or cast our palms at his feet. But we can honor him with our love and our gratitude for what he has done for us. Therefore, with hearts overflowing with thanksgiving, we offer our tithes and our offerings. Bless them, we pray, in the name of our triumphant Lord. Amen.

THE BENEDICTION

Follow your King this day! Receive grace and courage to complete your Lenten journey as you follow him to Gethsemane and Calvary. Then rise triumphant with him, as children whose robes have been washed in the blood of the Lamb. Amen.

CHRIST: OUR EXAMPLE IN HUMILITY

Lectionary:

Matthew 21:1-11	Triumphant entry
Philippians 2:5-11	Christ humbled himself
Isaiah 50:1-9a	He submitted to humiliation

Notes:
"A" — angel in charge of placements. Uses a laptop computer.

"B" — the preacher

B: *(Reads the texts for the day and ends with the Philippians reading)*
Today I want to discuss vocations — primarily the vocation of Jesus — and how his vocation affects our choice of vocation. You see, Jesus — even though he was equal with God — chose the vocation of a "servant." He actually gave up his princely status and became a "commoner."

A: *(Wanders in absent-mindedly, glasses down on his nose, intently working at the laptop he/she is carrying)*
Hmmm ... yep ... uh huh. *(Walks right into the pastor)* Oh, I beg your pardon. *(Begins to dust off the pastor)* Did I cause you harm? Dear me! Gracious me! This is no way for us to meet. He's probably going to speak to me about my "bungling" again.

B: "Bungling?" Who's he? And who are you?

A: *(Fixes his glasses up on his nose, juggles the laptop in one hand and extends the other hand to the pastor)* My name is Randichia *(ran-de-ki-ah),* but you can call me "Randy." I'm one of the Heavenly Host and I'm down here on assignment.

B: Heavenly Host? You mean you're an Angel?

A: That's right, that's right. *(Nearly drops his laptop as he fumbles to push his glasses up on his face again)* I became so interested in your topic that I forgot to keep myself invisible. Now that you have seen me, I guess there's not much point to hiding.

B: You are interested in today's sermon topic? Why?

A: You see, I'm the Angel-of-Placements. My job is to find the right person for the job — or is it the right job for the person? Oh well, that's what I do. And since you are going to talk about vocations, naturally I am very interested in what you will have to say.

B: Tell me, Randy, did you have anything to do with the placement of Jesus when he came to earth?

A: Welllll, indirectly. You see, I selected the carpentry vocation for Joseph, and when Jesus grew, he also learned to be a carpenter, and uh, er, that is, uh, I helped with the selection of one of Jesus' vocations.

B: And what about his call to preach and heal?

A: Let me see ... *(quickly types something into his laptop and reads the information out loud)* Nope, that was his own doing. To be perfectly honest with you *(peers over his glasses at the pastor)* I wasn't in favor of Jesus coming to earth in the first place. The Son of God has no business associating with mortals. He has more important things to do.

B: Oh? What would *you* have him do?

A: Well! *(Again types something into his laptop and reads the information out loud)* There is a new galaxy that is in the nebulous stage and it is *ripe* for completion. He could create a few more planets and stars and get them in motion. *(Grins broadly as he appears pleased with his answer)*

B: Have you spoken to God about this, Randy? Does he know how you feel about Jesus becoming a servant?

A: Oh my, yes. But, I'm just an angel and God is God. He's the Boss and it is *my* vocation to do as he tells me. Anyway, it happened. Jesus left heaven. He took off his royal robes and left his crown sitting on his throne. He gave up all that glory just so he could become a mortal. So what did you mortals do to the Son of God? You abused him. You arrested him. You executed him, and you put him in a tomb.

Now I ask you: Is that any way to treat the Son of God?

B: Now I understand why you were not in favor of Jesus coming to our planet earth. You are right. We mortals behaved in the worst possible way to the Son of God.

A: And from what I see *(indicates his laptop)* you continue to mistreat God's Son.

B: *(Addresses the congregation)* I'm sorry, people. I was going to preach a sermon; instead I am being interrogated. *(Turns his attention back to Randy)* Randy, I'm not going to defend the human race. You are absolutely correct in your judgment about the way people treat God's Son.

However, there is one thing I need to point out to you. In fact, you should already know this, considering you are an angel. Jesus *gave* up his life. No mortal could have the power to take his life. Jesus faced death because he loved us so much he was willing to die for us.

A: *(Sighs audibly)* Oh, I know you are right. But if you knew the Son of God like we know him, you would never have done to him such cruel things.

B: Those who did the cruel things were persons who did *not* know him. They had no idea that he was God's Son.

A: I don't know why they didn't; after all, he told them who he was.

B: Again, you are right. He did tell them, but only a few of them believed who he was.

A: *(Sarcastically)* Oh? Is that so? What about all those people who waved their palm branches *(waves his laptop over his head)*. They were so excited about making him king. That was quite a following, you know. What happened to all of them?

B: Sadly, I guess I have to say they were a mob out of control. It is true that they were hoping that Jesus would be their king, but still, they did *not* know who he was.

A: Pastor, you still have not convinced me that Jesus chose the right vocation! Why? *Why* did he do it?

B: There is only one reason: He did it because he loves us. The Son of God came to earth to show us what God was like. Sometimes I become confused about the real vocation of Jesus: Was it to show us what God was like? Or was it to become the sacrificial lamb for the sins of the world?

A: *(Quickly types into his laptop)* The answer is: *both!* According to my listing of placements, the one vocation cannot be separated from the other.

B: So! That means if Jesus was showing us God, it was God who died on that cross. God himself became our sacrifice!

A: Ahh, it would appear so. But you see, my laptop is not equipped to find a vocation for God. Everything was created to serve God; *we're* the ones who need vocations.

B: Don't you find that to be wonderful? We were created to love and serve God, yet he came and served us!

A: Yes, it is rather remarkable. The King of Kings humbling himself, exposing himself to the common cold and measles, walking about on foot from city to city, *(With a show of contempt)* riding a jackass ... Do you people appreciate what the Son of God has done for you?

B: Oh, yes!! Some of us do! That's why we seek vocations that will honor his intentions for humankind.

A: And that, my friend, is *my* job. If you want to find out the vocation in which each person should be employed, just check with me. I even know what the little baby in the *(third)* pew should do when he grows up.

B: Would you tell us?

A: Nope! That's against the rules. God and I are allowed to know. God programmed the computer, you know, but I am not allowed to divulge this information to anyone.

B: Then how are people to know what their vocations should be?

A: You forget. I am an angel, and there are many angels that are working to help people discover their vocation. But, ultimately, you mortals have a power which we angels do not have.

B: Oh? And what might that be?

A: You mortals have the right to choose. God created you with a will. Unless you surrender that will to God, chances are you will never accept the vocation God has planned for you.

B: That's because God created us in his image; he gave us a will because he has a will.

A: *(Shakes his head sadly)* A bad mistake, a baaaad mistake!

B: Obviously God did not think so.

A: That's because he has more confidence in you than I have. Too bad you let him down.

B: So Jesus humbled himself and surrendered his will to God and accepted the only vocation that could possibly win over the hearts and souls of us mortals.

A: And if Jesus was so willing to be humbled, why is it that you mortals cannot follow his example?

B: You mean, be willing to die as Jesus did?

A: *(Impatiently)* No, no! I mean be humble enough to *serve* one another! Be humble enough to do it for Jesus' sake. He did it for you. Why can't you do it for him?

B: Hold on there, Randy. That's my vocation! You're doing the preaching. Remember? You're in charge of placements.

A: All right. I apologize. So go ahead and preach!

B: *(Addressing the congregation)* My friends, Randy is right. If the Son of God was willing to humble himself and accept mortality that we may come to know what God is like, what right do we have to be so proud? Not one of us can honestly say we are perfect. Not one of us is really worthy of what he willingly did for us.

The Good News is that he did it for us out of love. God loves each one of us so much that he provided us a way to find forgiveness and new life.

This week we will commemorate the passion and death of our Lord. Our *Lord!* Not just some man named Jesus. Our Lord willingly submitted himself to be our sacrifice. He died in our stead for the sins we commit.

If we would receive this forgiveness, let us humble ourselves to ask for it. He will not withhold it from us. After all, that's why he came to earth in the first place, because he loves us and wants us to enter into his kingdom of truth and love.

A: *(Takes off his glasses and wipes a tear from his eyes)* Pastor, you make me wish that I could be a mortal. Oh, how much Jesus loved you. I guess he chose the right vocation after all.

B: Randy, perhaps angels serve God because they are programmed to do so; or perhaps they serve him because they love him. The amazing thing is that Jesus served us! He did it because he loves us. He did not have to die for you angels, but he chose to die for us.

(To congregation) Finally, my friends, I ask that you not only humble yourselves and ask for forgiveness. I also ask that you follow his way and discover your vocation in him. Whatever you do for him, you can be certain it will be something special.

Let us pray:

Almighty God, we humbly approach your throne and give honor and glory to your Son, Jesus, the Christ, who again reigns with you in power and glory. We may not be worthy of such great love, but that doesn't change the fact that we are indeed loved by you. Thank you for this great love and grace. Have mercy on us and teach us to walk humbly with you. Amen.

A TENEBRAE CHANCEL DRAMA

WHAT TIME IS IT?

Setting And Special Effects

A long table is placed in the center of the chancel. It may be covered with a white or purple cloth. In the very center should be a large Christ candle. On either side of this candle should be the twelve apostle candles (six to a side). Let the acolytes light the candles prior to the drama, beginning with the Christ candle.

The Apostles should process in, slowly, during the singing of the hymn, " 'Tis Midnight, And On Olive's Brow," and take their places around three sides of the table, leaving the front vacant. They should stand throughout the drama, heads bowed low, with hands clasped in front.

The Apostles could be in choir robes, and each should have a shawl or scarf covering the head, hanging down as though it was a monk's hood, shielding the face from view.

The Narrator should read from the lectern, and may also be dressed as a monk.

The sanctuary lights should be dimmed, and only the chancel lights should shine down on the Apostles; or a blue floodlight could be trained on the scene. As the drama progresses, the chancel lights should grow dimmer with each segment, and finally be darkened at the end of the drama.

As the Narrator introduces each segment of the drama, a chime is sounded (either on the organ or a handbell). The chime is tolled once, then twice, then three times, and so forth, until all twelve Apostles are gone. It should be tolled slowly.

Participants

Narrator
12 Apostles (may be men and women and/or youth)
Acolyte(s)
Bell ringer
Light effects person

(All scripture references are from the *New Revised Standard Version*.)

76

Narrator may stand at a lectern to read his (or) her lines, either behind the Apostles or to the side of the Apostles.

Let the first part of the worship service proceed up to the singing of the hymn, " 'Tis Midnight, And On Olive's Brow." During the singing of this hymn, let the Apostles process slowly to their places behind the table with the lighted candles.

Dim the sanctuary lights.

Narrator: What time is it? It is time to follow Jesus.

(One chime is heard.)

Narrator: *(Reads Matthew 4:18-25)* "As (Jesus) walked by the Sea of Galilee, he saw two brothers, Simon, who is called Peter, and Andrew his brother, casting a net into the sea — for they were fishermen. And he said to them, 'Follow me, and I will make you fish for people.' Immediately they left their nets and followed him. As he went from there, he saw two other brothers, James son of Zebedee and his brother John, in the boat with their father Zebedee, mending their nets, and he called them. Immediately they left the boat and their father, and followed him.

"Jesus went throughout Galilee, teaching in their synagogues and proclaiming the good news of the kingdom and curing every disease and every sickness among the people. So his fame spread throughout all Syria, and they brought to him all the sick, those who were afflicted with various diseases and pains, demoniacs, epileptics, and paralytics, and he cured them. And great crowds followed him from Galilee, the Decapolis, Jerusalem, Judea, and from beyond the Jordan."

Following a leader such as Christ Jesus is difficult. Even the most faithful will fall behind and follow from a distance. Look! One is disenchanted already; his name is Judas. He goes to sell out his Lord!

Apostle 1 (Judas): *(Raises head very slowly to look at the audience. He holds a money bag in his hands.)* I have been following him for three years, and nothing has happened. Every coin we receive is given to the poor. How can we establish a government (kingdom, he calls it) without anything in our treasury? The treasury is my responsibility What a joke!

The priests are right. He's not the Messiah. It's about time I ended this charade and exposed him as a fraud! I think I'll pay a visit to the home of the high priest tonight.

(Apostle 1 exits down the main aisle, and the Acolyte extinguishes one of the candles.)

Narrator: What time is it? Time to receive Christ's freedom!

(Two chimes, played slowly, are heard.)

Narrator: *(Reads John 8:31-36)* "Then Jesus said to the Jews who had believed in him, 'If you continue in my word, you are truly my disciples; and you will know the truth, and the truth will make you free.' They answered him, 'We are descendants of Abraham and have never been slaves to anyone. What do you mean by saying, "You will be made free"?'

"Jesus answered them, 'Very truly, I tell you, everyone who commits sin is a slave to sin. The slave does not have a permanent place in the household; the Son has a place there forever. So if the Son makes you free, you will be free indeed.' "

Certainly, with the offer of freedom, Christ will have *many* followers!

Apostle 2: *(Slowly raises head and addresses audience.)* Freedom? I don't feel free. I feel closed in. Everywhere we go I'm on the defensive. They're out there *(looks suspiciously over his shoulder as he talks)* just waiting for us. I tried to convince Jesus to set up a secret headquarters so their spies won't hear everything. We may just have to take this operation underground. I thought everyone wanted the Messiah to come, but I guess not. Obviously we have an uphill struggle on our hands to fight the hierarchy. I'm going to find me a good place to hide 'til this is all over.

(Apostle 2 exits and Acolyte extinguishes second candle.)

Narrator: What time is it? It is time to recognize Jesus for what and who he is.

(Three chimes are slowly played.)

Narrator: *(Reads John 7:25-26, 31)* "Now some of the people of Jerusalem were saying, 'Is not this the man whom they are trying to kill? And here he is, speaking openly, but they say nothing to him! Can it be that the authorities really know that this is the Messiah?'

"Yet many in the crowd believed in him and were saying, 'When the Messiah comes, will he do more signs than this man has done?'"

Ah! Now that more people are ready to believe that Jesus is the Messiah, surely he will have *faithful* followers.

Apostle 3: *(Raises head very slowly and addresses the audience.)* I followed Jesus because John the Baptist said: "He is the *one*; he's the Messiah." I must admit that he is different from any man I've ever known. He talks like a leader; he assumes authority to such a degree that our religious leaders feel threatened. But I still don't know ... shouldn't something dramatic happen? Like overthrowing the present government? I just don't know ... *(Wags head slowly as he walks away.)*

(Apostle 3 exits and Acolyte extinguishes third candle.)

Narrator: What time is it? It is time to learn of Jesus.

(Four chimes are slowly played.)

Narrator: *(Reads Matthew 5:38-48)* Jesus taught the people. "You have heard that it was said, 'An eye for an eye and a tooth for a tooth.' But I say to you, do not resist an evildoer. If anyone strikes you on the right cheek, turn the other also; and if anyone wants to

79

sue you and take your coat, give your cloak as well; and if anyone forces you to go one mile, go also the second mile. Give to everyone who begs from you, and do not refuse anyone who wants to borrow from you.

"You have heard that it was said, 'You shall love your neighbor and hate your enemy.' But I say to you, love your enemies and pray for those who persecute you, so that you may be children of your Father in heaven; for he makes his sun rise on the evil and on the good, and sends rain on the righteous and on the unrighteous. For if you love those who love you, what reward do you have? Do not even the tax collectors do the same? And if you greet only your brothers and sisters, what more are you doing than others? Do not even the Gentiles do the same? Be perfect, therefore, as your heavenly Father is perfect."

Jesus is obviously a revolutionary leader, for his teachings are unique ... even contrary to what the people have always believed. What effect will these teachings have upon his followers?

Apostle 4: *(Raises head very slowly and addresses the audience.)* Everywhere we go crowds of people follow us. They can't get enough of his teachings. Or is it the *miracles* he does? Hmph! Probably the miracles — because his teachings are *hard*. I'm afraid not many can enter his kingdom if they have to be perfect. I'm not perfect. Is he waiting until we become perfect? The kingdom will never come at that requirement. And to think I left my wife for three years — for what?

(Apostle 4 exits and Acolyte extinguishes fourth candle.)

Narrator: What time is it? It is time for equal rights.

(Five chimes are slowly played.)

Narrator: *(Reads Mark 10:11-16)* "Jesus said to them, 'Whoever divorces his wife and marries another commits adultery against her; and if she divorces her husband and marries another, she commits adultery.'

80

"People were bringing little children to him in order that he might touch them; and the disciples spoke sternly to them. But when Jesus saw this, he was indignant, and said to them, 'Let the little children come to me; do not stop them; for it is to such as these that the kingdom of God belongs. Truly I tell you, whoever does not receive the kingdom of God as a little child will never enter it.' And he took them up in his arms, laid his hands on them, and blessed them."

In all we read of Jesus, it can be noted that he treated women as equal to men. We also read that he elevated children as supreme examples of trust and belief.

Apostle 5: *(Raises head very slowly and addresses the audience.)* Hmph! I was really embarrassed that day when I tried to send the kids and their mothers along their way. Couldn't Jesus see that I was only trying to protect him? Trying to give him a little rest? This business about the kingdom being filled with children — I don't know. What kind of a kingdom will it be to have noisy kids running all over? Who's going to want to put up with that?

(Apostle 5 exits and Acolyte extinguishes fifth candle.)

Narrator: What time is it? It is time to take the offensive!

(Six chimes are slowly played.)

Narrator: *(Reads John 12:12-13, 17-19, 37)* "The next day the great crowd that had come to the festival heard that Jesus was coming to Jerusalem. So they took branches of palm trees and went out to meet him, shouting, 'Hosanna! Blessed is the one who comes in the name of the Lord, the King of Israel!'

"So the crowd that had been with him when he called Lazarus out of the tomb and raised him from the dead continued to testify. It was also because they heard that he had performed this sign that the crowd went to meet him. The Pharisees then said to one another, 'You see, you can do nothing. Look, the world has gone after him!'

"Although he had performed so many signs in their presence, they did not believe in him."

The Master deliberately rode into the middle of a hornet's nest and faced those who were against him. "All the world" was following him; the ball was in his court and it seemed he was mounting the offensive against the enemy.

Apostle 6: *(Raises head very slowly and addresses the audience.)* We Zealots had been waiting for such a day as that great triumphant entry into the capital city. The Roman dogs didn't know what was happening, but I could tell they were nervous. Even the Jewish leaders were afraid of a riot.

But nothing happened. Right then and there, Jesus could have taken over the kingdom! Right then and there he had the people in his control and they would have made him their king.

But nothing happened! I followed him because I thought he would be our deliverer — but nothing happened ...

(Apostle 6 exits and Acolyte extinguishes sixth candle.)

Narrator: What time is it? It is time to follow his example.

(Seven chimes are slowly played.)

Narrator: *(Reads John 13:3-9, 12-15)* "Jesus, knowing that the Father had given all things into his hands, and that he had come from God and was going to God, got up from the table, took off his outer robe, and tied a towel around himself. Then he poured water into a basin and began to wash the disciples' feet and to wipe them with the towel that was tied around him. He came to Simon Peter, who said to him, 'Lord, are you going to wash my feet?' Jesus answered, 'You do not know now what I am doing, but later you will understand.'"

"Peter said to him, 'You will never wash my feet.' Jesus answered, 'Unless I wash you, you have no share with me.' Simon Peter said to him, 'Lord, not my feet only, but also my hands and my head!'

82

"After he had washed their feet, had put on his robe, and had returned to the table, he said to them, 'Do you know what I have done to you? You call me Teacher and Lord — and you are right, for that is what I am. So if I, your Lord and Teacher, have washed your feet, you also ought to wash one another's feet. For I have set you an example, that you also should do as I have done to you.' "

The Master became the servant. He knew he was the Son of God; yet he humbly washed the feet of his disciples, explaining that he was "setting them an example" in behavior.

Apostle 7: *(Raises head very slowly and addresses the audience.)* I think I was the only man who was intelligent enough to realize that the Master didn't belong on his knees washing our feet! If the rest of the guys had protested, we could have reversed things. We could have washed *his* feet. But I guess I wasn't intelligent enough to get the idea at the beginning. I guess I didn't have enough love.

(Apostle 7 exits and Acolyte extinguishes seventh candle.)

Narrator: What time is it? It is time to learn a new commandment.

(Eight chimes are slowly played.)

Narrator: *(Reads John 13:33-35; 14:15)* "(Jesus said,) 'Little children, I am with you only a little longer. You will look for me; and as I said to the Jews, so now I say to you, "Where I am going, you cannot come." I give you a new commandment, that you love one another. Just as I have loved you, you also should love one another. By this everyone will know that you are my disciples, if you have love for one another.'

" 'If you love me, you will keep my commandments.' "

Jesus knew that love cannot be commanded. But he also knew that the Jewish mentality understood the "commandment concept." They were good by commandment, but not from inward purity.

Apostle 8: *(Raises head very slowly and addresses the audience.)* The Master was always teaching us something new; we came to expect this. Perhaps we were a little too close to him. Maybe we became too accustomed to his words. Or maybe he knew what was really going on among us. I can't honestly say that there was a great deal of love among the bunch of us. Some of us were obviously a little superior, and there were those who resented it.

He was right. If there was one thing we needed, it was love. I can't bear to face him now ...

(Apostle 8 exits and Acolyte extinguishes eighth candle.)

Narrator: What time is it? It is time to begin the Lord's memorial.

(Nine chimes are slowly played.)

Narrator: *(Reads Luke 22:7-8, 14, 19-22)* "Then came the day of unleavened bread, on which the Passover lamb had to be sacrificed. So Jesus sent Peter and John, saying, 'Go and prepare the Passover meal for us that we may eat it.'

"When the hour came, he took his place at the table, and the apostles with him ... Then he took a loaf of bread, and when he had given thanks, he broke it and gave it to them, saying, 'This is my body, which is given for you. Do this in remembrance of me.' And he did the same with the cup after supper, saying, 'This cup that is poured out for you is the new covenant in my blood. But see, the one who betrays me is with me, and his hand is on the table. For the Son of Man is going as it has been determined, but woe to that one by whom he is betrayed!' "

I must confess that if I had been present at that meal, I would have been very confused by the memorial ritual which Jesus established that night.

Apostle 9: *(Raises head very slowly and addresses the audience.)* Symbolic rituals were not new to us Jews. Everything which we ate during that Passover meal was a symbol of suffering, to remind us that we were rescued from bondage in Egypt and delivered by the angel of death. But our law strictly forbids us to drink the blood of an animal, let alone a human. Confused? Yes, we were!

I never understood that he was actually going to give up *his* blood for the sins of the world. I was really expecting things to go a little differently.

(Apostle 9 exits and Acolyte extinguishes ninth candle.)

Narrator: What time is it? It is time to pray.

(Ten chimes are slowly played.)

Narrator: *(Reads Mark 14:32-40)* "They went to a place called Gethsemane; and he said to his disciples, 'Sit here while I pray.' He took with him Peter and James and John, and began to be distressed and agitated. And he said to them, 'I am deeply grieved, even to death; remain here, and keep awake.' And going a little farther, he threw himself on the ground and prayed that, if it were possible, the hour might pass from him. He said, 'Abba, Father, for you all things are possible; remove this cup from me; yet, not what I want, but what you want.'

"He came and found them sleeping, and he said to Peter, 'Simon, are you asleep? Could you not keep awake one hour? Keep awake and pray that you may not come into the time of trial; the spirit indeed is willing, but the flesh is weak.'

"And again he went away and prayed, saying the same words. And once more he came and found them sleeping, for their eyes were very heavy; and they did not know what to say to him."

By this time the apostles must have sensed some of the anguish of their Master. Why didn't they join him in prayer?

Apostle 10: *(Raises head very slowly and addresses the audience.)* Of course we sensed that Jesus was troubled. We were not completely unfeeling. But we were human, after all. It had been a long day; we shared a good meal and some wine; we were tired. That doesn't excuse us.

In reality, we just were not tuned in to the seriousness of his situation. He performed so many miracles, and I felt confident that he could get out of any predicament. My falling asleep didn't mean that I didn't care ...

(Apostle 10 exits and Acolyte extinguishes tenth candle.)

Narrator: What time is it? It is time to be betrayed.

(Eleven chimes are slowly played.)

Narrator: *(Reads Mark 14:41-46; 15:16-20)* "When Jesus came a third time (after praying) he said to them, 'Are you still sleeping and taking your rest? Enough! The hour has come; the Son of Man is betrayed into the hands of sinners. Get up, let us be going. See, my betrayer is at hand.'

"While he was still speaking, Judas, one of the twelve, arrived; and with him there was a crowd with swords and clubs, from the chief priests, the scribes, and the elders. Now the betrayer had given them a sign, saying, 'The one I will kiss is the man; arrest him and lead him away under guard.' So when he came, he went up to him at once and said, 'Rabbi!' and kissed him. Then they laid hands on him and arrested him.

"Then the soldiers led him into the courtyard of the palace (that is, the governor's headquarters); and they called together the whole cohort. And they clothed him in a purple cloak; and after twisting some thorns into a crown, they put it on him, and they began saluting him, 'Hail, King of the Jews!' They struck his head with a reed, spat upon him, and knelt down in homage to him. After mocking him, they stripped him of the purple cloak and put his own clothes on him. Then they led him out to crucify him."

Betrayed by one of his own! Judas may have brought about the dastardly deed, but somehow I feel that Jesus was betrayed by all his disciples.

Apostle 11: *(Raises head very slowly and addresses the audience.)* So much happened, and so fast! One minute we were quietly praying in the garden; the next minute we were surrounded by soldiers from the temple! A few of us tried to defend the Master and we drew our weapons. But he wouldn't let us fight! He told us to put our weapons away.

If you can't fight, there are only two other recourses: one is to be captured, the other is to retreat. I'm not dumb; I retreated!

(Apostle 11 exits and Acolyte extinguishes eleventh candle.)

Narrator: What time is it? It is time to hear the prophecy fulfilled.

(Twelve chimes are slowly played.)

Narrator: *(Reads Isaiah 53:3-6)* "He was despised and rejected by others; a man of suffering and acquainted with infirmity; and as one from whom others hide their faces he was despised, and we held him of no account.

"Surely he has borne our infirmities and carried our diseases; yet we accounted him stricken, struck down by God, and afflicted. But he was wounded for our transgressions, crushed for our iniquities; upon him was the punishment that made us whole, and by his bruises we are healed.

"All we like sheep have gone astray; we have turned to our own way, and the Lord has laid on him the iniquity of us all."

Is it possible that someone would have remembered those words from Isaiah? Perhaps they never truly understood what those words meant.

Apostle 12: *(Raises head very slowly and addresses the audience.)* Perhaps the one who *did* understand the meaning of those words was the mother of Jesus. I stood with her at the foot of the cross, stunned and bewildered. She was brokenhearted and wept bitterly.

It was all over. Our hopes, our dreams for the kingdom. They executed our leader. How quickly my world dissolved around me.

(Apostle 12 exits and Acolyte extinguishes twelfth candle.)

Narrator: What time is it? It is time to die.

(Thirteen chimes are slowly played.)

Narrator: *(Reads Luke 23:44-47; 24:46-48)* "And it was now about noon, and darkness came over the whole land until three in the afternoon, while the sun's light failed; and the curtain of the temple was torn in two. Then Jesus, crying with a loud voice, said, 'Father, into your hands I commend my spirit.' Having said this, he breathed his last.

"When the centurion saw what had taken place, he praised God and said, 'Certainly this man was innocent.'

"Thus it is written, that the Messiah is to suffer and to rise from the dead on the third day, and that repentance and forgiveness of sins is to be proclaimed in his name to all nations, beginning from Jerusalem. You are witnesses of these things."

(Narrator walks to the table and lifts the Christ candle, turns around and slowly exits down the main aisle of the sanctuary, carrying the lighted Christ candle.)

The house lights are turned on, very slowly, to allow the darkness to penetrate the psyche of the audience.

The organ (or the congregation or soloist) may play/sing verses 1, 2, and 5 of "Were You There?" at the conclusion of the drama.

www.ingramcontent.com/pod-product-compliance
Lightning Source LLC
Chambersburg PA
CBHW071017040426
42443CB00007B/819